D0772576

AMBULANCE RESCUE

EMERGENCY VEHICLES

Deborah Chancellor

A$^+$

Smart Apple Media

Published by Smart Apple Media,
an imprint of Black Rabbit Books
P.O. Box 3263, Mankato, Minnesota 56002
www.blackrabbitbooks.com

Published by arrangement with the Watts Publishing
Group LTD, London.

Library of Congress Cataloging-in-Publication Data
Chancellor, Deborah.
 Ambulance rescue / by Deborah Chancellor.
   pages cm. — (Emergency vehicles)
 Includes index.
 Summary: "Introduces readers to eight different
ambulance rescue vehicles, such as helicopters and army
ambulances, and explains how each emergency vehicle
is used by paramedics to help injured people in different
situations. Includes a reading quiz and web sites"—
Provided by publisher.
 ISBN 978-1-59920-888-6 (library binding)
1. Ambulance service—Juvenile literature.
2. Ambulances—Juvenile literature. 3. Emergency
medicine—Juvenile literature. I. Title.
 RA995.C43 2014
 362.18'8—Adc23
                        2012040044

Printed in the United States and Corporate Graphics,
North Mankato, Minnesota.

PO1585
2-2013

9 8 7 6 5 4 3 2 1

Series editor: Adrian Cole/Amy Stephenson
Editor: Sarah Ridley
Art direction: Peter Scoulding
Designer: Steve Prosser
Picture researcher: Diana Morris

Picture credits:
Avico Ltd/Alamy: 15t.
Stuart Clarke/Rex Features: 19t.
Ashley Cooper/Alamy: 12-13, 13t.
Ian Danbury/Dreamstime: 18-19.
Gary Dobner/Alamy: 11.
Fire Photo/Alamy: 9t.
A Wesley Floyd/Shutterstock: 5t.
Image Source/Rex Features: 6.
Timothy Large/Dreamstime: 8-9.
Dennis MacDonald/Alamy: 4.
Travis Manley/istockphoto: front cover, 5b.
Roberto Marinello/Dreamstime: 7.
Bruce Miller/Alamy: 16.
one-image photography/Alamy: 10.
Realimage/Alamy: 14-15.
Royal Flying Doctor Service: 17.
Tupungato/Shutterstock: 21t.
Zmiel Photography/istockphoto: 20-21.

Every attempt has been made to clear copyright.
Should there be any inadvertent omission,
please apply to the publisher for rectification.

BEEEEP!

Contents

Flashing Lights

Ambulances carry sick or injured people to the hospital. This ambulance is speeding to an emergency. Lights flash and **sirens** wail.

WHOOEE!

The "star of life" **symbol** appears on many ambulances around the world. It shows that they belong to the emergency medical services.

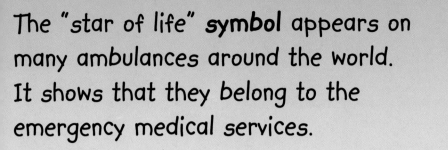

Flashing lights

Star of life

AMBULANCE

Emergency Care

The ambulance crew members are called **paramedics**. They use a **stretcher** to put a patient into the ambulance.

Paramedics are trained to do emergency first aid. They can use all the life-saving **equipment** on board the ambulance.

Blood pressure equipment

Equipment for broken limbs

Patient safety belt

Stretcher

Breathing equipment

7

Rapid Reaction

A fast paramedic car rushes to an accident. The paramedics use the **two-way radio** to call for more ambulances if they are needed.

WHOOOEEEE!

The front of the car has the word "AMBULANCE" written on it backwards. Drivers read the word in their mirrors and then know to move out of the way. →

AMBULANCE SERVICE

VROOOOOOM!

Traffic Buster

A speedy paramedic motorcycle zips through crowded streets to reach an emergency. **Panniers** on the motorcycle carry life-saving equipment.

The motorcycle helmet has a two-way radio.

BEEEEP! BEEEEP!

The bright colors and flashing lights on a paramedic motorcycle make it easy to spot on the road.

PARAMEDIC

Rough Ride

Sturdy off-road ambulances are built to drive over rough ground. The heavy tire **tread** keeps the ambulance from skidding.

BBRRRR!

AMBULANCE

nk E. Mellor

A searchlight on the ambulance's **hood** helps find injured people at night.

RRR!

Airlift

A helicopter that flies sick people to the hospital is called an air ambulance. Important medical equipment is kept on board.

An air ambulance can fly to places that cannot be reached any other way.

CHUPPPA!

WHUPPPA!

Flying Doctor

Some people who live far from towns and cities need planes to bring doctors and nurses to them.

VROOOOOMM!

EEOOOOOWW!

This patient needs to be flown to a hospital far away. The plane's crew of doctors and nurses will care for him during the long flight.

Battle Zone

An army ambulance is covered with strong metal **plates** to protect it from bullets, **mines**, and explosions.

CHUPPPA!

WHUPPPA!

WHUPPPA!

CHUPPPA!

63

The **Red Cross** symbol tells the enemy that this is an ambulance.

Armies use air ambulances to fly injured soldiers out of **war zones**.

Emergency Boat

Colorful speedboats are used as ambulances in places where water is the quickest way to travel.

AZIEND
ULS

AMBULANZA

SPLASH!

A siren warns other boats to move out of the way. The boat carries medical equipment and trained staff to care for patients.

BRUUMMM!

ZIANA

KODEN

6V 23573

AMBULANZA

Glossary

blood pressure the force of blood pushing on the sides of the tubes that carry blood around your body

emergency a sudden or dangerous event or situation

equipment the items you need to do something

hood the cover over a vehicle's engine

mines bombs hidden under the ground

panniers boxes or bags on the back of a bike

paramedics people who are trained to do emergency first aid

plates protective metal armor

Red Cross an organization that protects people in danger

sirens a loud hooting or wailing sound

stretcher a bed with handles for carrying sick or injured people

symbol a picture or thing that stands for something else

tread the patterns on a rubber tire

two-way radio a radio set you use to talk to somebody far away

war zones dangerous places where battles are fought

Quiz

1. Why is the word "AMBULANCE" often written backwards on an ambulance?

2. What are paramedics?

3. Why do ambulances display the "star of life" symbol?

4. What is kept in the panniers on a paramedic motorcycle?

5. What is an air ambulance?

6. How are army ambulances protected from attack?

Index

Web Sites

www.911forkids.com/

encyclopedia.kids.net.au/page/pa/Paramedic

Kidshealth.org/Kid/watch/er/911.html

WHOOEE!